THE LIMITS OF SURVIVAL

SANDSTORM TERROR!

Desert Survivor

BY **James Buckley Jr.**

ILLUSTRATED BY **Cassie Anderson**

BEARPORT
PUBLISHING

Minneapolis, Minnesota

BEAR CLAW

Credits

Cover art by Cassie Anderson

Photos: 20T © Billion Photos/Shutterstock; 20B © Oleg Troino/Shutterstock; 21T © New Africa/Shutterstock; 21B © Susan Schmitz/Shutterstock; 22T © Jon Manjeot/Shutterstock; 22B © JeniFoto; 23T © Andrew Rapp/Shutterstock; 23B © Frantic00/Shutterstock.

Bearport Publishing Company Product Development Team

President: Jen Jenson; Director of Product Development: Spencer Brinker; Senior Editor: Allison Juda; Editor: Charly Haley; Associate Editor: Naomi Reich; Senior Designer: Colin O'Dea; Associate Designer: Elena Klinkner; Product Development Assistant: Anita Stasson

Produced by Shoreline Publishing Group LLC
Santa Barbara, California
Designer: Patty Kelley
Editorial Director: James Buckley Jr.

DISCLAIMER: This graphic story is a dramatization based on true events. It is intended to give the reader a sense of the narrative rather than a presentation of actual details as they occurred.

Library of Congress Cataloging-in-Publication Data

Names: Buckley, James, Jr., 1963- author. | Anderson, Cassie, illustrator.
Title: Sandstorm terror! : desert survivor / by James Buckley Jr. ;
    illustrated by Cassie Anderson.
Description: Minneapolis, Minnesota : Bearport Publishing, 2023. | Series:
    The limits of survival | "Bear claw". | Includes bibliographical
    references and index.
Identifiers: LCCN 2022002324 (print) | LCCN 2022002325 (ebook) | ISBN
    9781636919911 (library binding) | ISBN 9781636919980 (paperback) | ISBN
    9798885090056 (ebook)
Subjects: LCSH: Prosperi, Mauro, 1955---Comic books, strips, etc. |
    Marathon des sables--Comic books, strips, etc. | Desert
    survival--Morocco--Comic books, strips, etc. | Sandstorms--Comic books,
    strips, etc. | Long distance runners--Italy--Comic books, strips, etc. |
    Graphic novels.
Classification: LCC GV1061.15.P76 B84 2023 (print) | LCC GV1061.15.P76
    (ebook) | DDC 613.6/9--dc23/eng/20220223
LC record available at https://lccn.loc.gov/2022002324
LC ebook record available at https://lccn.loc.gov/2022002325

For more information, write to Bearport Publishing, 5357 Penn Avenue South, Minneapolis, MN 55419. Printed in the United States of America.

CONTENTS

Chapter 1
Dangerous Race

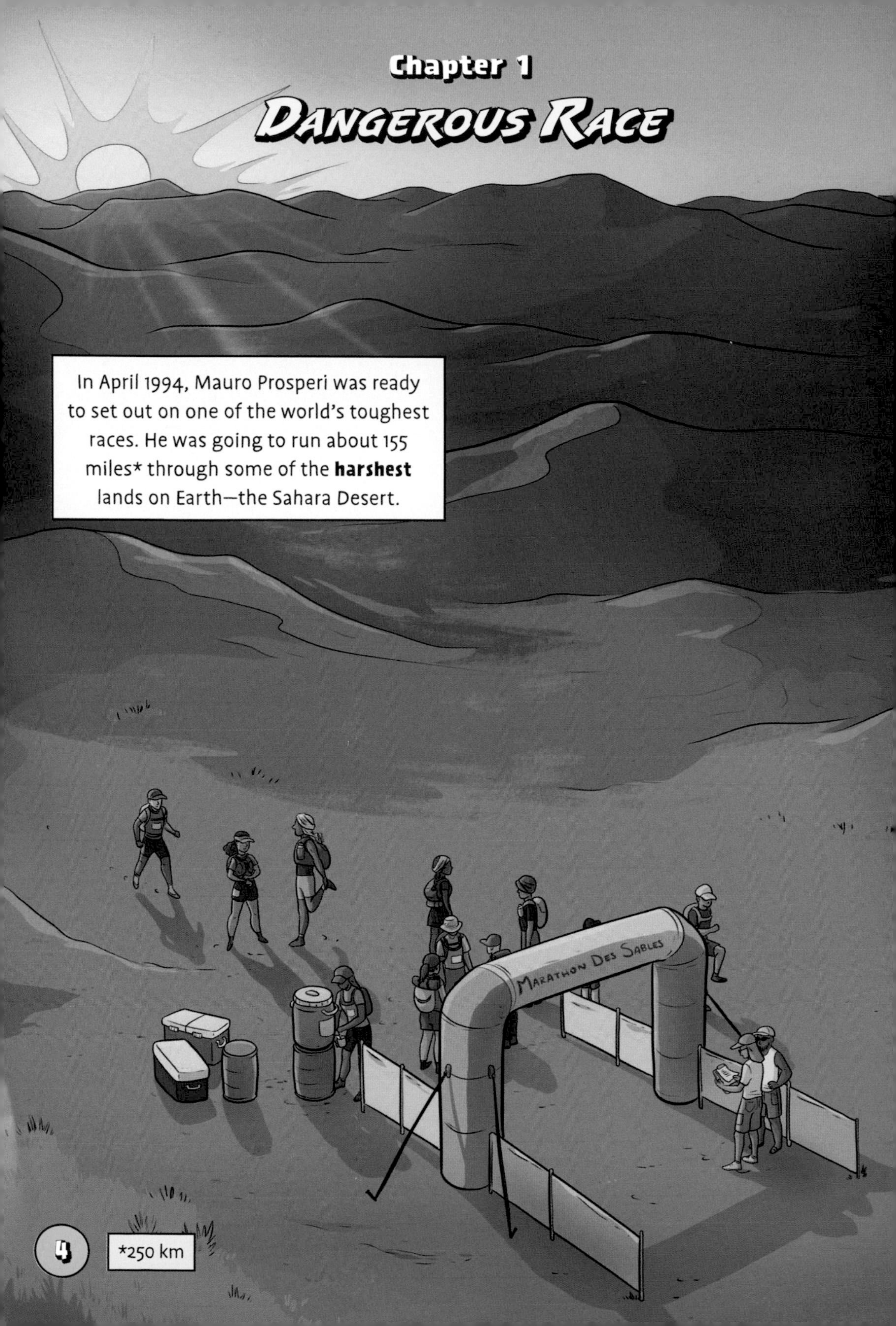
In April 1994, Mauro Prosperi was ready to set out on one of the world's toughest races. He was going to run about 155 miles* through some of the **harshest** lands on Earth—the Sahara Desert.
Marathon Des Sables

*250 km

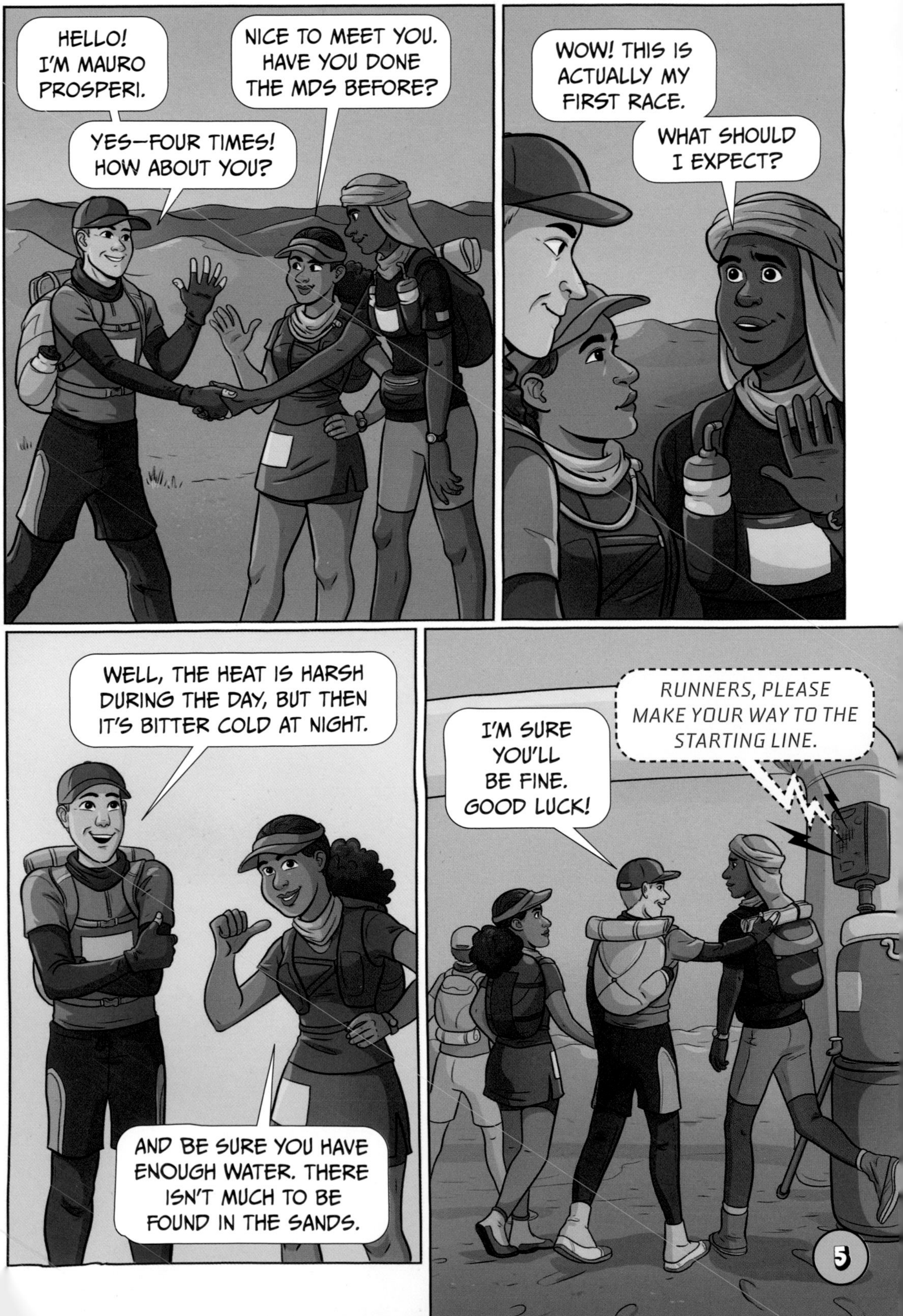
HELLO! I'M MAURO PROSPERI.
NICE TO MEET YOU. HAVE YOU DONE THE MDS BEFORE?
YES—FOUR TIMES! HOW ABOUT YOU?
WOW! THIS IS ACTUALLY MY FIRST RACE.
WHAT SHOULD I EXPECT?
WELL, THE HEAT IS HARSH DURING THE DAY, BUT THEN IT'S BITTER COLD AT NIGHT.
AND BE SURE YOU HAVE ENOUGH WATER. THERE ISN'T MUCH TO BE FOUND IN THE SANDS.
I'M SURE YOU'LL BE FINE. GOOD LUCK!
RUNNERS, PLEASE MAKE YOUR WAY TO THE STARTING LINE.

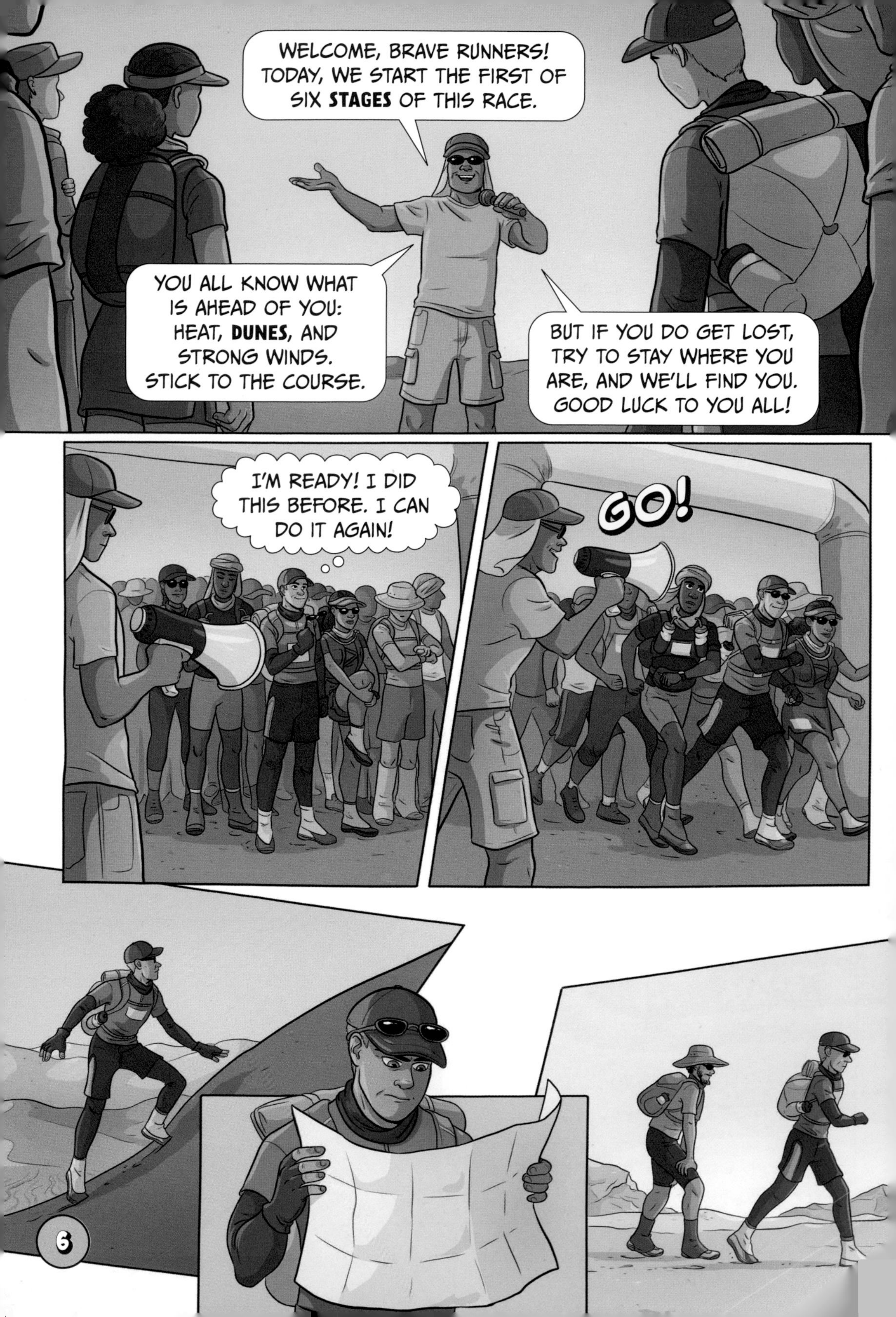
WELCOME, BRAVE RUNNERS! TODAY, WE START THE FIRST OF SIX **STAGES** OF THIS RACE.
YOU ALL KNOW WHAT IS AHEAD OF YOU: HEAT, **DUNES**, AND STRONG WINDS. STICK TO THE COURSE.
BUT IF YOU DO GET LOST, TRY TO STAY WHERE YOU ARE, AND WE'LL FIND YOU. GOOD LUCK TO YOU ALL!
I'M READY! I DID THIS BEFORE. I CAN DO IT AGAIN!
GO!

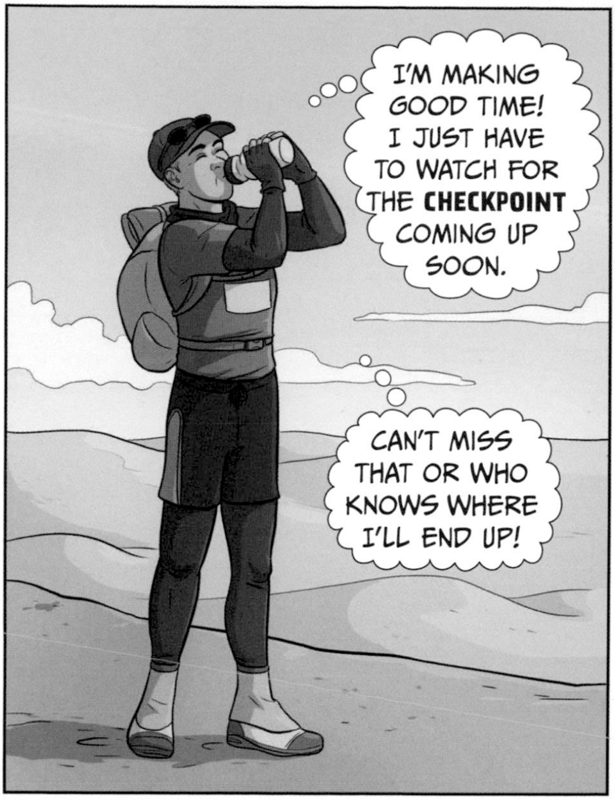
I'M MAKING GOOD TIME! I JUST HAVE TO WATCH FOR THE **CHECKPOINT** COMING UP SOON.
CAN'T MISS THAT OR WHO KNOWS WHERE I'LL END UP!

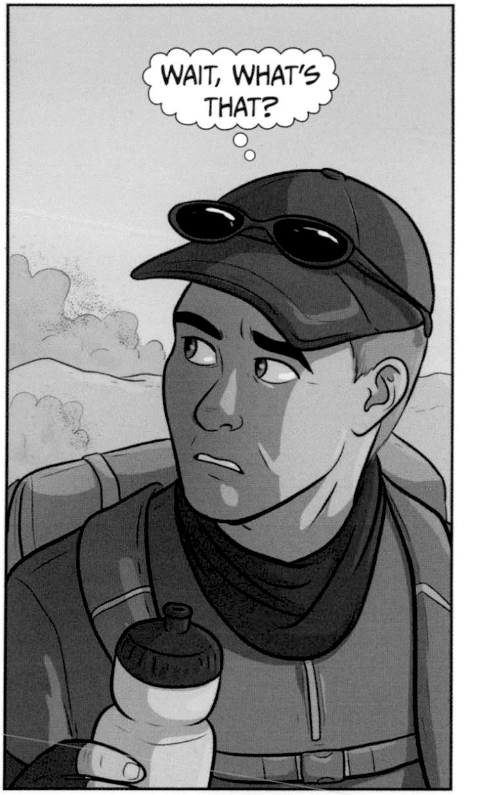
WAIT, WHAT'S THAT?

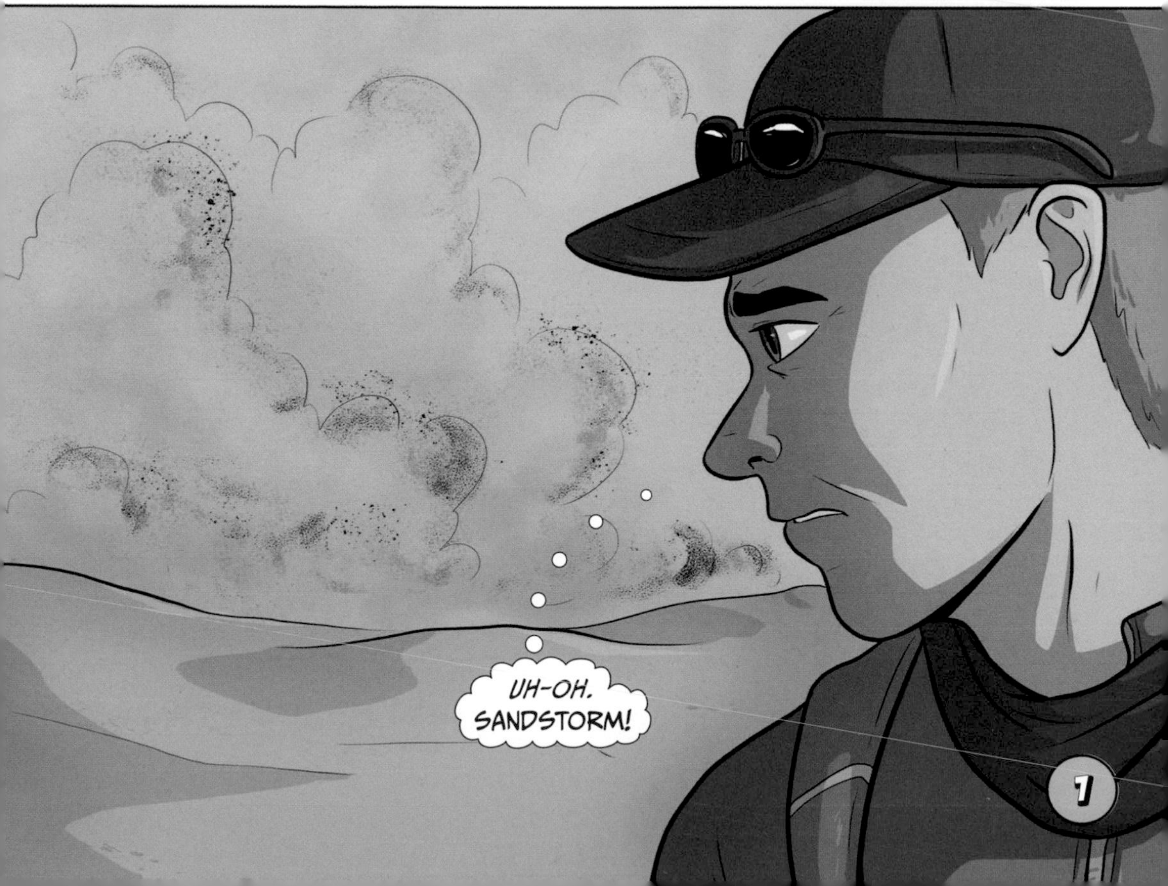
UH-OH. SANDSTORM!

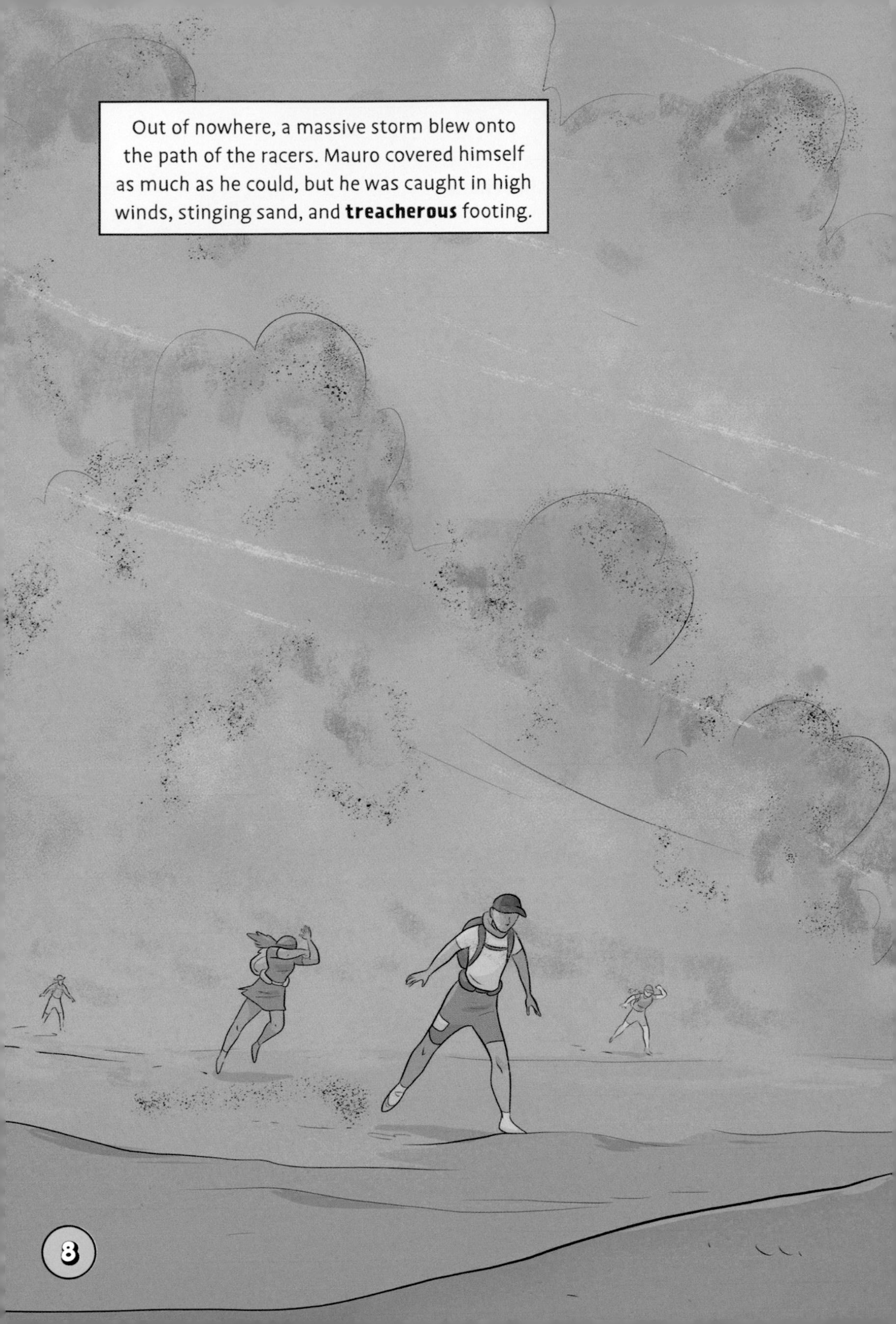
Out of nowhere, a massive storm blew onto the path of the racers. Mauro covered himself as much as he could, but he was caught in high winds, stinging sand, and **treacherous** footing.

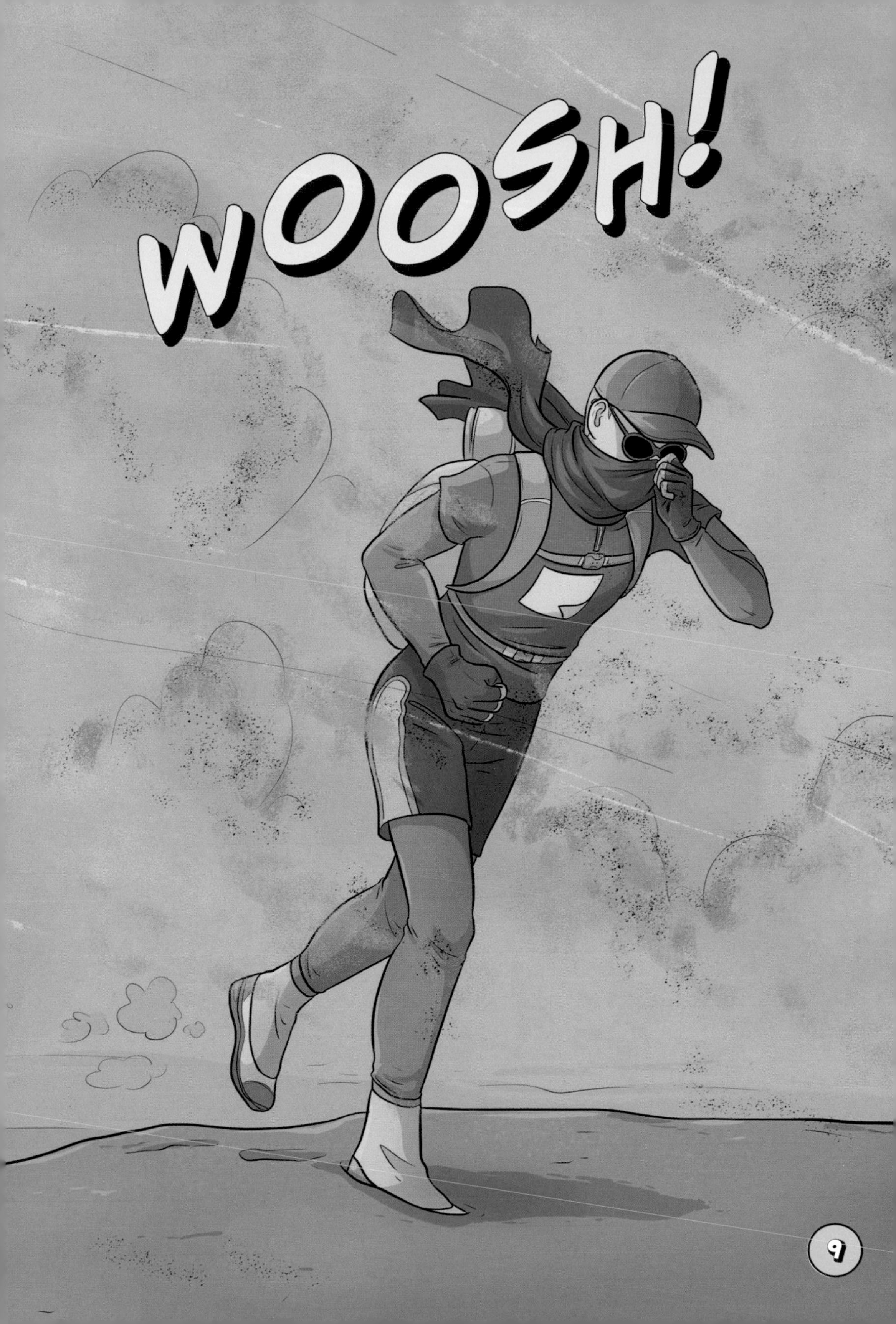
WOOSH!

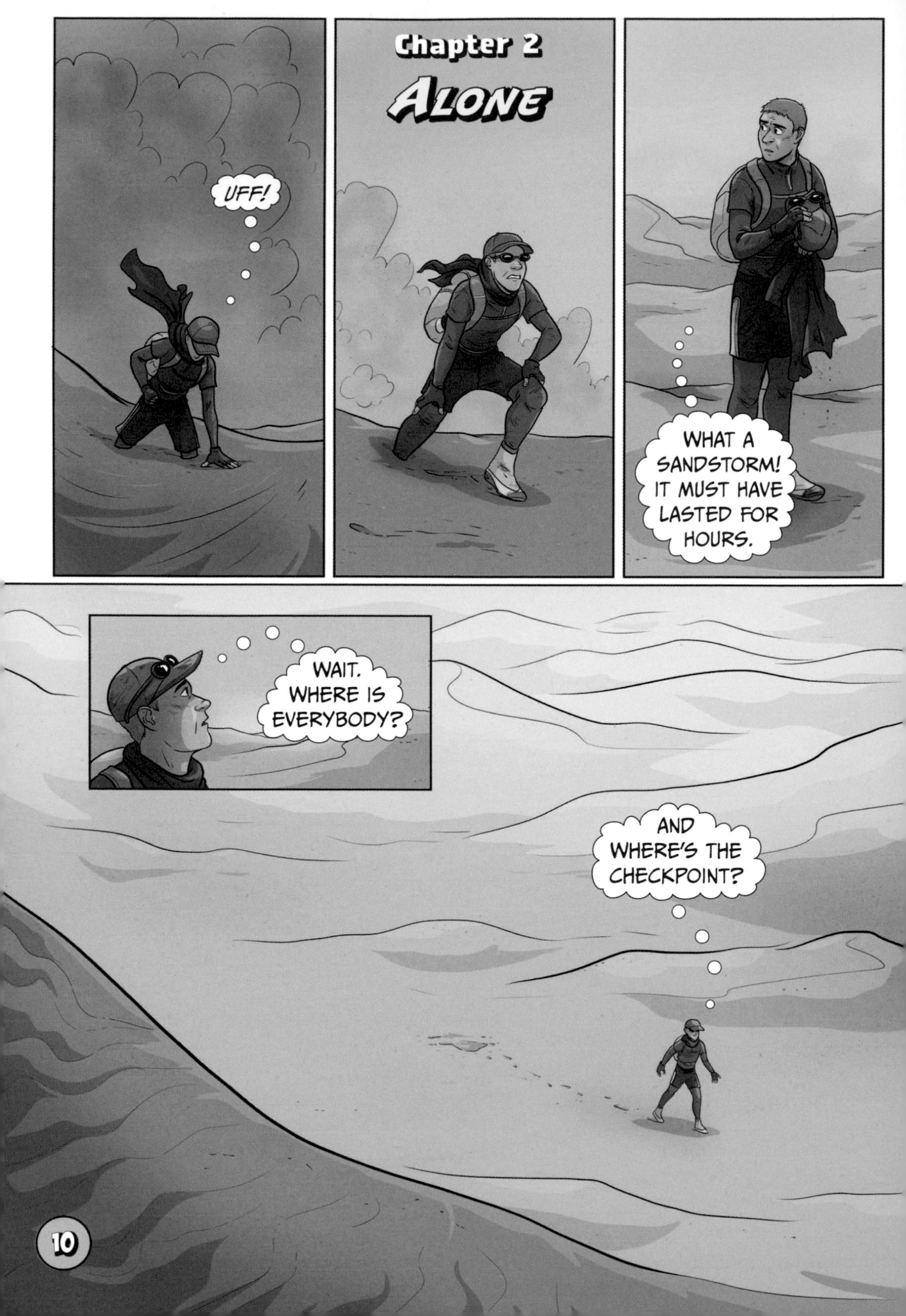
UFF!
Chapter 2
ALONE
WHAT A SANDSTORM! IT MUST HAVE LASTED FOR HOURS.
WAIT. WHERE IS EVERYBODY?
AND WHERE'S THE CHECKPOINT?

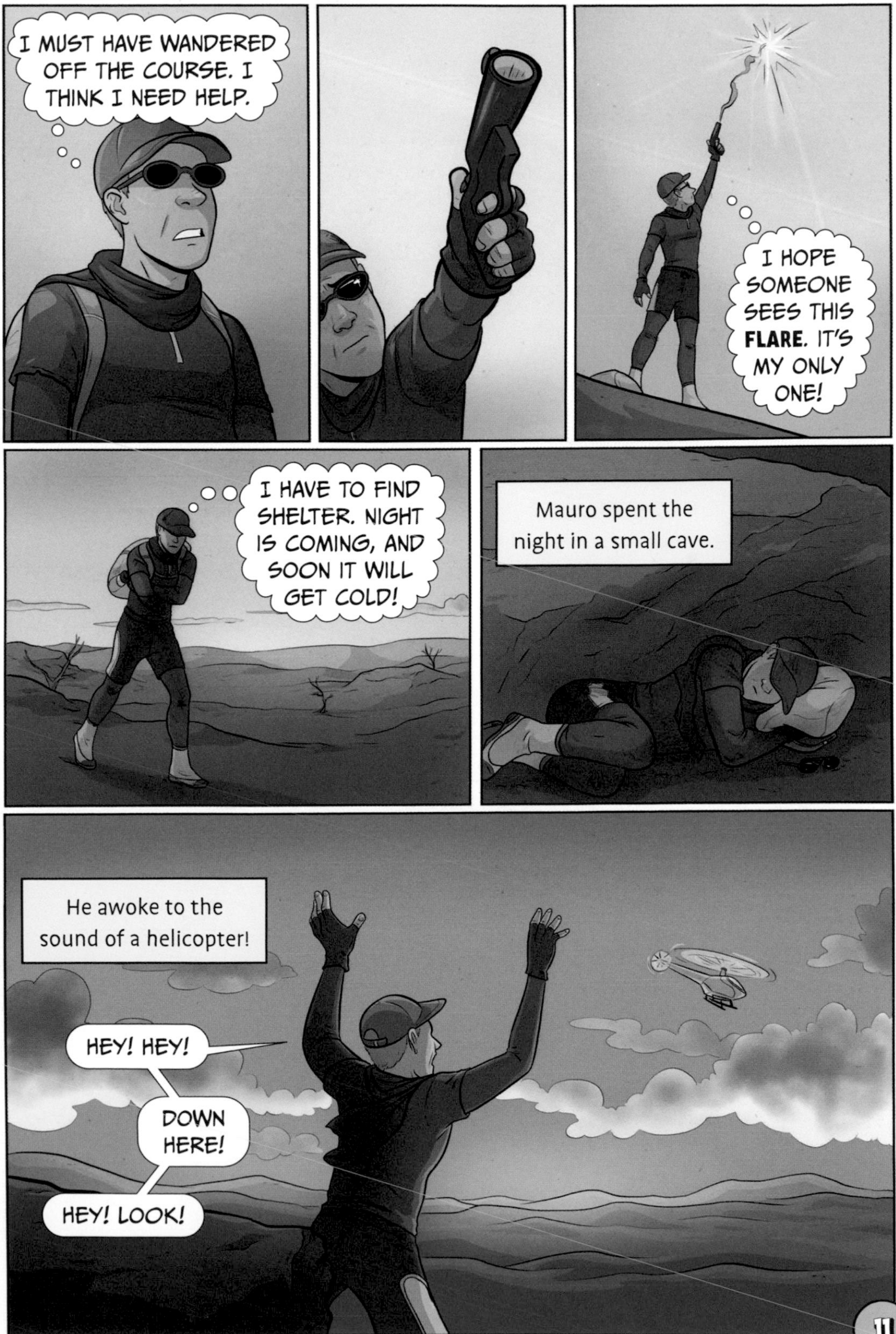
I MUST HAVE WANDERED OFF THE COURSE. I THINK I NEED HELP.
I HOPE SOMEONE SEES THIS **FLARE.** IT'S MY ONLY ONE!
I HAVE TO FIND SHELTER. NIGHT IS COMING, AND SOON IT WILL GET COLD!
Mauro spent the night in a small cave.
He awoke to the sound of a helicopter!
HEY! HEY!
DOWN HERE!
HEY! LOOK!

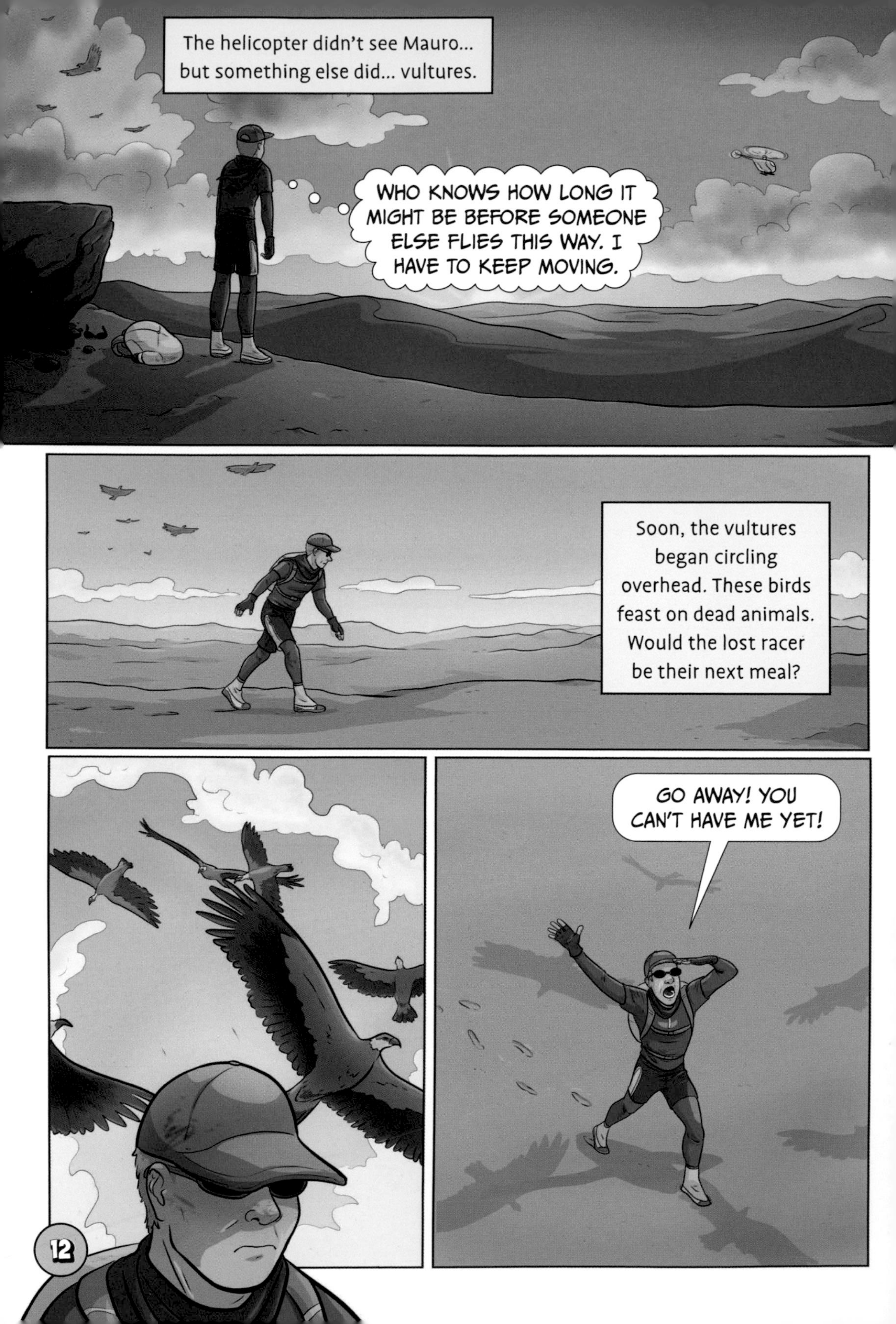
The helicopter didn't see Mauro... but something else did... vultures.
WHO KNOWS HOW LONG IT MIGHT BE BEFORE SOMEONE ELSE FLIES THIS WAY. I HAVE TO KEEP MOVING.
Soon, the vultures began circling overhead. These birds feast on dead animals. Would the lost racer be their next meal?
GO AWAY! YOU CAN'T HAVE ME YET!

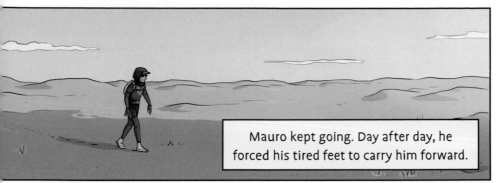

Mauro kept going. Day after day, he forced his tired feet to carry him forward.

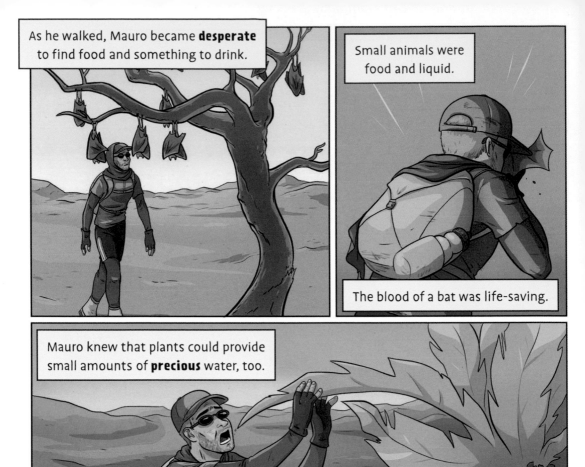

As he walked, Mauro became **desperate** to find food and something to drink.

Small animals were food and liquid.

The blood of a bat was life-saving.

Mauro knew that plants could provide small amounts of **precious** water, too.

Each night, he had to find a way to stay warm. When the sun went down, the temperature **plummeted**.

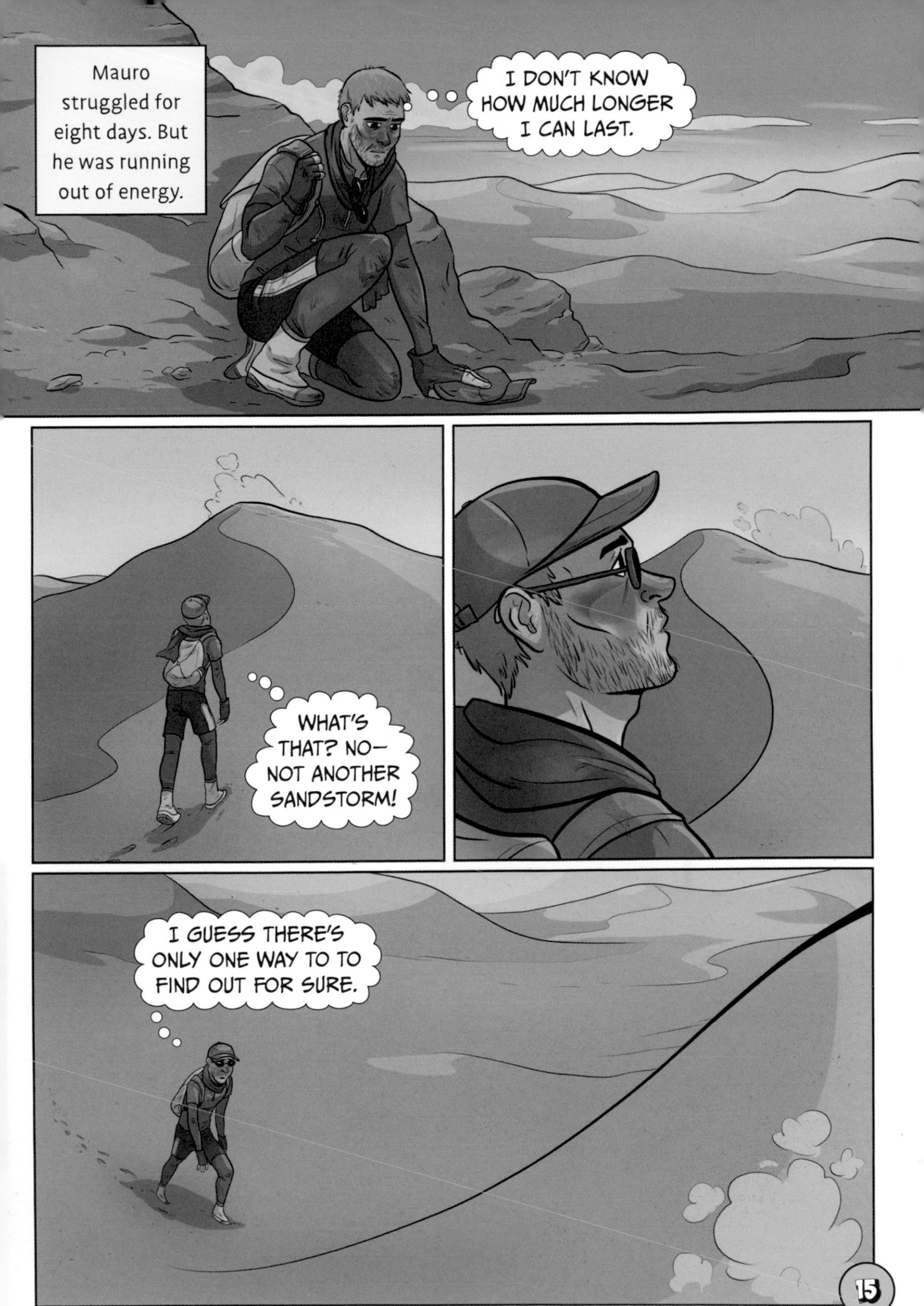
Mauro struggled for eight days. But he was running out of energy.
I DON'T KNOW HOW MUCH LONGER I CAN LAST.
WHAT'S THAT? NO— NOT ANOTHER SANDSTORM!
I GUESS THERE'S ONLY ONE WAY TO TO FIND OUT FOR SURE.

Chapter 3

RESCUE!

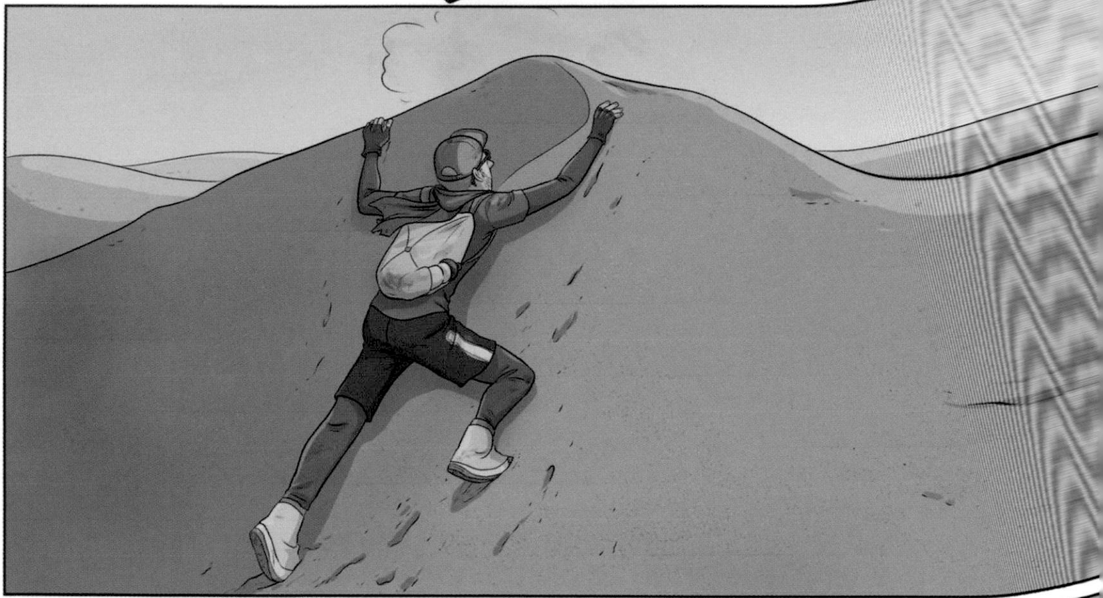

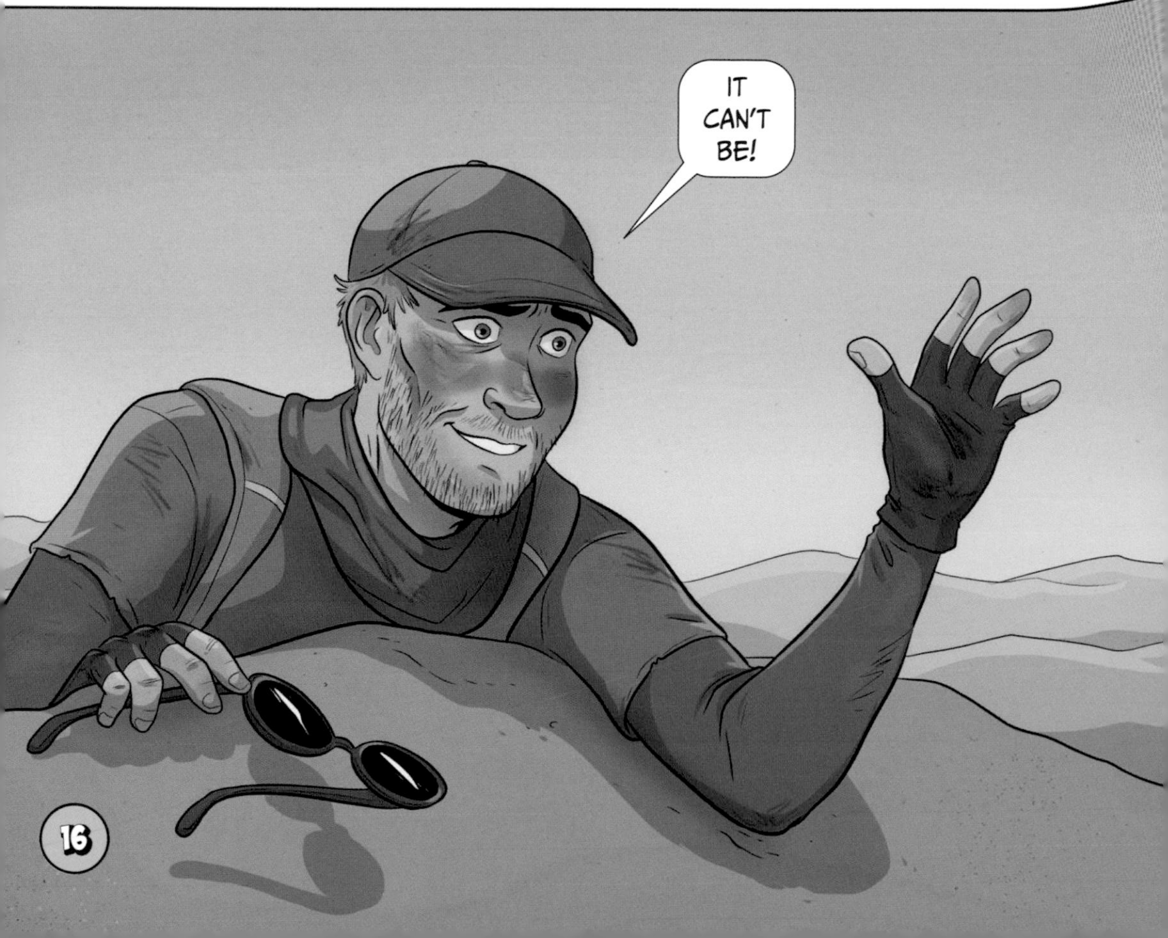
IT CAN'T BE!

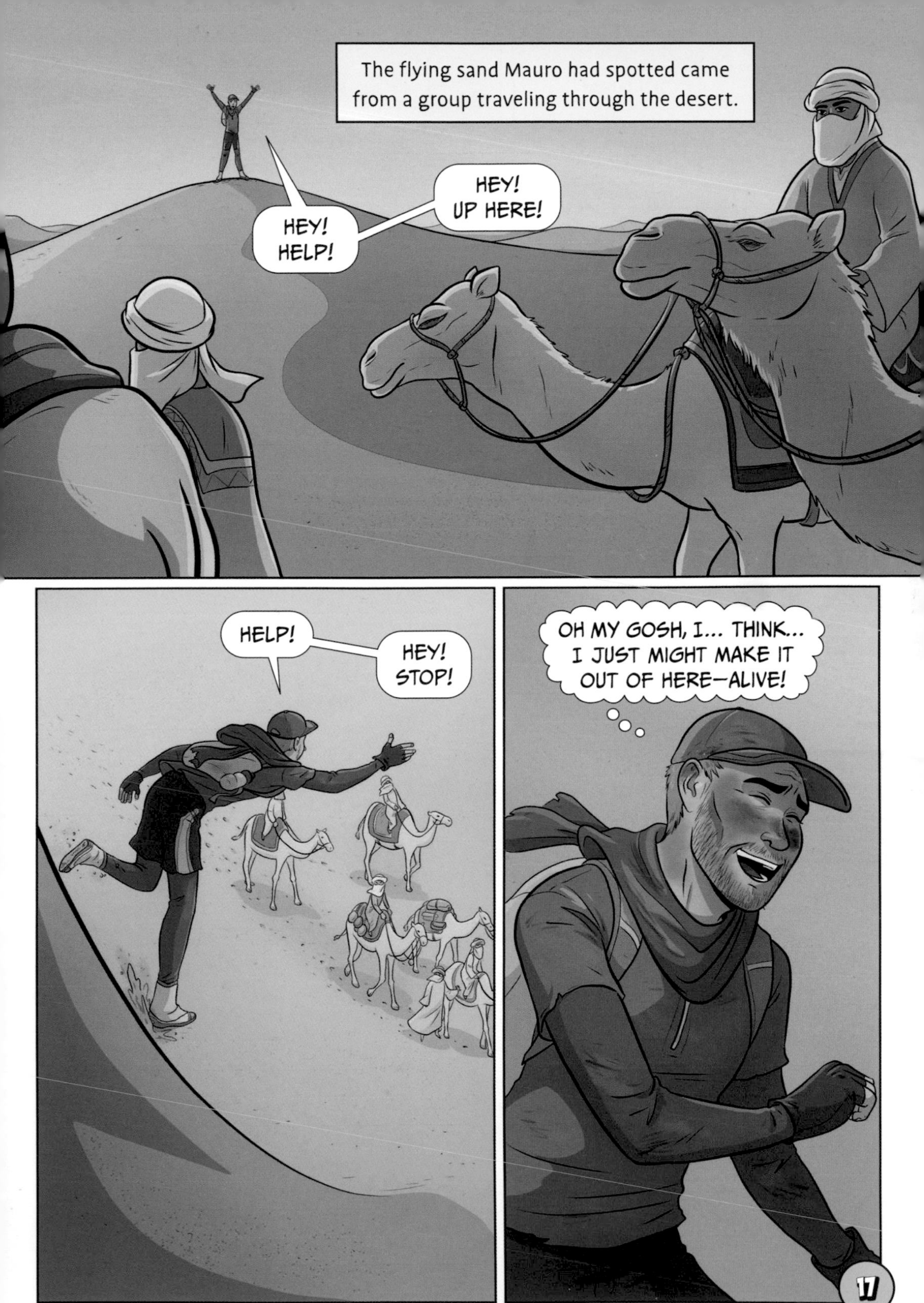
The flying sand Mauro had spotted came from a group traveling through the desert.
HEY! HELP!
HEY! UP HERE!
HELP!
HEY! STOP!
OH MY GOSH, I... THINK... I JUST MIGHT MAKE IT OUT OF HERE—ALIVE!

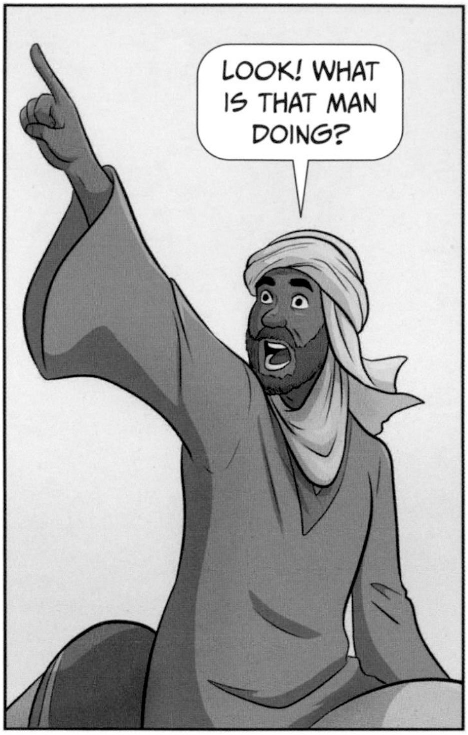
LOOK! WHAT IS THAT MAN DOING?

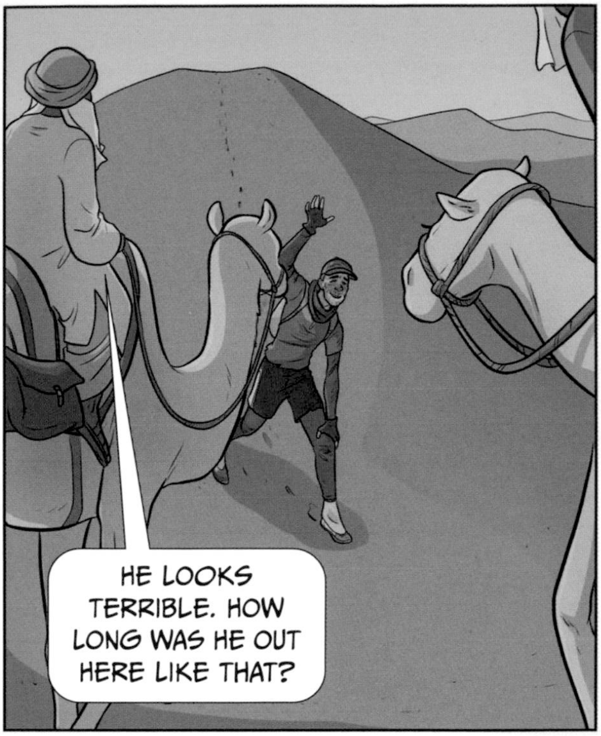
HE LOOKS TERRIBLE. HOW LONG WAS HE OUT HERE LIKE THAT?

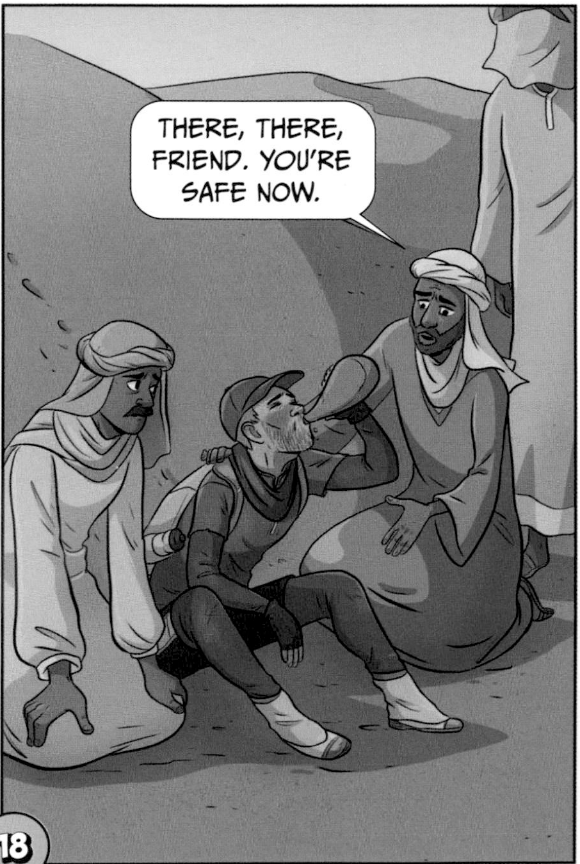
THERE, THERE, FRIEND. YOU'RE SAFE NOW.

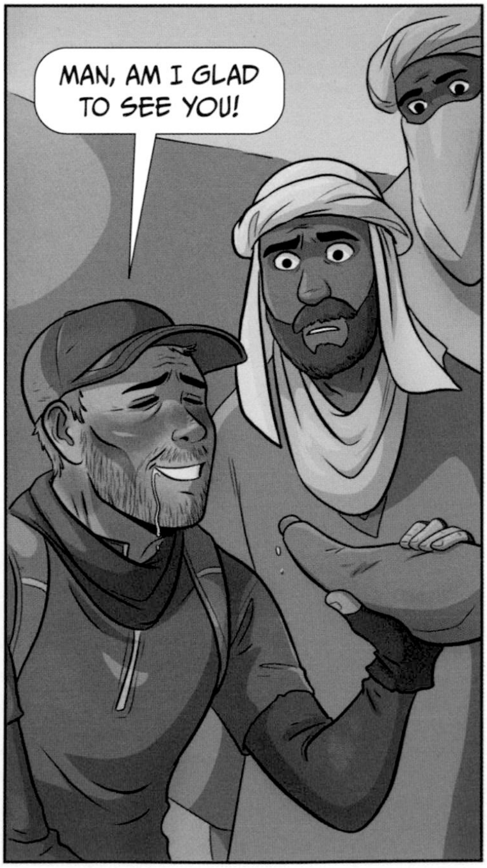
MAN, AM I GLAD TO SEE YOU!

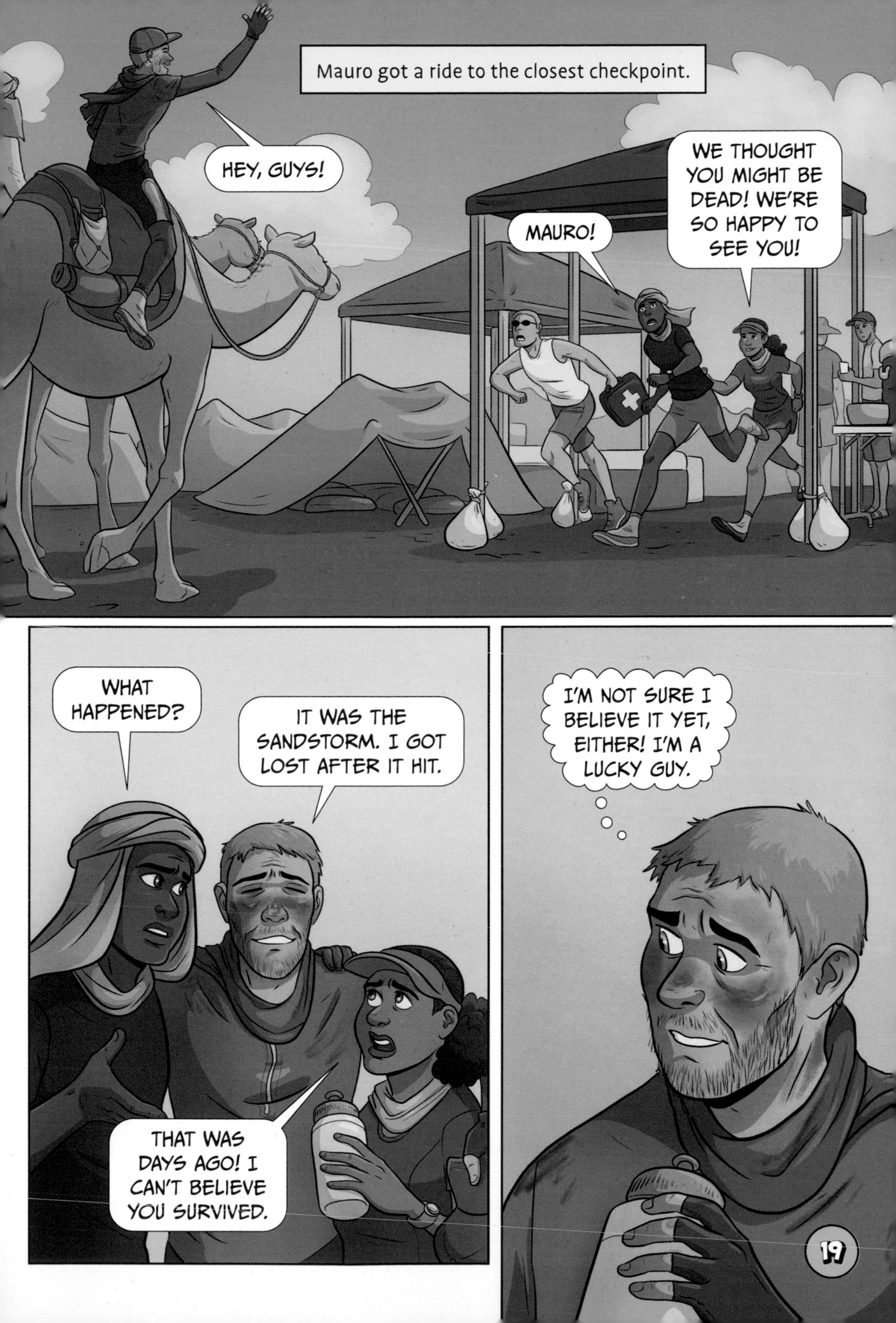

Mauro got a ride to the closest checkpoint.
HEY, GUYS!
MAURO!
WE THOUGHT YOU MIGHT BE DEAD! WE'RE SO HAPPY TO SEE YOU!
WHAT HAPPENED?
IT WAS THE SANDSTORM. I GOT LOST AFTER IT HIT.
THAT WAS DAYS AGO! I CAN'T BELIEVE YOU SURVIVED.
I'M NOT SURE I BELIEVE IT YET, EITHER! I'M A LUCKY GUY.

DESERT SURVIVAL TIPS

If you plan to visit a desert, follow these tips to help you survive.

➕ Before you go, tell people where you are traveling and when you plan to return.

➕ Bring a cell phone with plenty of power.

➕ Carry extra food and water in case you find yourself out for longer than expected.

➕ Bring enough clothing and a sleeping bag to stay warm during cold desert nights.

- Bring matches. You can start fires to stay warm and to let people know you need help.
- Find shade to protect yourself from the sun. If you must be out in the sun, wear sunscreen, a hat, light-colored clothing that covers your body, and sunglasses.

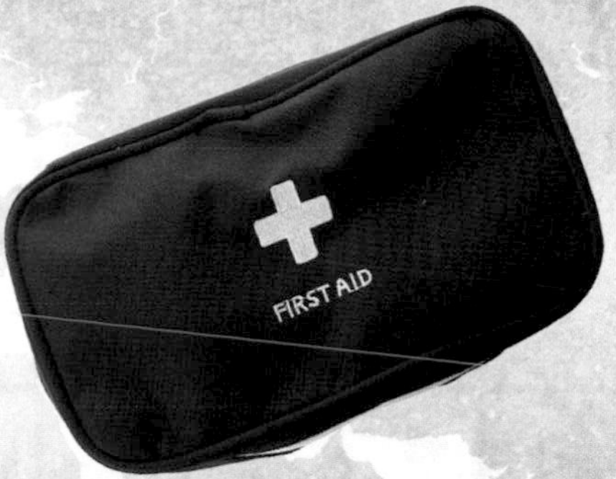
FIRST AID

- If a sandstorm occurs, close your eyes or put on glasses. Cover your nose and mouth with a cloth or handkerchief to protect your lungs from the sand. Keep your back to the wind so the sand doesn't blow directly in your face.
- In the desert heat, drink water regularly so you do not become **dehydrated**.
- Try to move in the early morning or just before it gets dark. During these times, it is cooler.
- Keep away from dangerous desert creatures such as spiders, scorpions, and snakes. Tuck your pant legs into your socks or shoes to decrease the chances of getting stung or bitten.

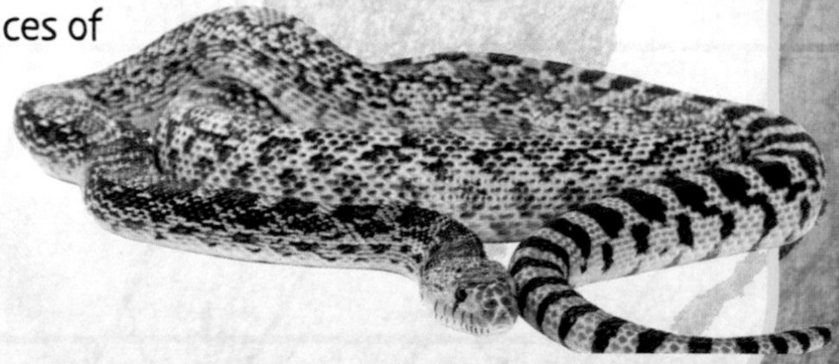

OTHER DESERT SURVIVORS

William LaFever was lost in the Arizona desert for more than three weeks. He had planned a 90-mile (145-km) hike but got lost. Soon, he had finished all the water he brought with him. He survived by drinking from a tiny river and catching frogs to eat. Finally, a rescue helicopter found him and brought him to safety.

Ann Rogers used her head when she got lost in a desert. When her car ran out of gas, she gathered all her gear and headed toward what she hoped was a town. Over the next nine days, she walked mile after mile in the heat. At one point, she made a huge sign in the sand. When a helicopter in search of her saw the sign, she was rescued.

Glossary

checkpoint a place where travelers must report as they make their way along a path

dehydrated lacking enough water or moisture

desperate feeling as if there is no hope

dunes large mounds of sand in a desert

flare a very bright light meant to attract attention

harshest most difficult or most dangerous

plummeted dropped rapidly

precious rare and important

stages sections of a race, by either time or distance

treacherous very dangerous or difficult

Index

Read More

Eason, Sarah. *Desert Survival Guide (Brave the Biome)*. New York: Crabtree, 2021.

Hayes, Vicki. *Surviving the Desert (Survival Stories)*. Minneapolis: Kaleidoscope, 2020.

Spradlin, Michael P. *Sandstorm Blast: A 4D Book (Pararescue Corps)*. North Mankato, MN: Stone Arch Books, 2019.

Learn More Online

1. Go to **www.factsurfer.com** or scan the QR code below.

2. Enter **"Sandstorm Terror"** into the search box.

3. Click on the cover of this book to see a list of websites.